Gems of Song

Also from Westphalia Press

westphaliapress.org

Gems of Song

for Eastern Star Chapters

Compiled by Pitkin & Mathews

WESTPHALIA PRESS
An imprint of Policy Studies Organization

Westphalia Press
An imprint of Policy Studies Organization
1527 New Hampshire Ave., NW
Washington, D.C. 20036
info@ipsonet.org

ISBN-13: 978-1633910249
ISBN-10: 1633910245

Cover design by Taillefer Long at Illuminated Stories:
www.illuminatedstories.com

Daniel Gutierrez-Sandoval, Executive Director
PSO and Westphalia Press

Devin Proctor, Director of Media and Publications
PSO and Westphalia Press

Updated material and comments on this edition
can be found at the Westphalia Press website:
www.westphaliapress.org

GEMS OF SONG

FOR

Eastern Star Chapters

COMPILED AND PUBLISHED BY

LORRAINE J. PITKIN AND JENNIE E. MATHEWS
1066 Berwyn Ave., Edgewater   ROCKFORD,
CHICAGO, ILL.   IOWA.

THIRTY-FIRST EDITION

Chicago, 1920

Price 70 cents

To the Members

of the

Order of the Eastern Star,

wherever dispersed, throughout
the Globe,

This Book is Dedicated.

GEMS OF SONG.

CORONATION. C. M.

Rob. Morris, LL. D.

Oliver Holden.

1. Be - hold, how pleas - ant and how good For sis-ters who a - gree,
2. On friend-ship's al - tar, ris - ing there, Our hands now plighted be,

Of the ac-cept-ed sis - ter-hood, To dwell in u - ni - ty.
To live in love with hearts sincere, In peace and u - ni - ty.

Of the ac-cept-ed sis - ter-hood to dwell in u - ni - ty.
To live in love with hearts sin-cere, In peace and u - ni - ty.

MARLOW.

1. With earnest hearts and will-ing hands, With-in our chap-ter room
2. To aid each oth - er on the way, Thro' maz es dark and drear;
3. That Star which shall the faith-ful guide Tho' long and drear the road,

We meet, a warm fra - ter - nal band, Our la - bors to re - sume.
While o'er us all the gold-en ray Of Bethlehem's Star shines clear.
To gild, at Life's fair ev - en-tide, The cit - y of our God!

BEDFORD.

1. With - in our Chapter met a - gain, With hearts and pur - pose strong,
2. Around our al-tar's sa - cred shrine, May Love's pure in - cense rise,

We'll raise our notes of grate - ful praise, With un-ion in our song.
Bear - ing up - on its mys - tic flame Our mu-sic to the skies.

STEPHENS. C. M.

W. Jones.

1. We will not grieve for pleas-ures gone, For bro-ken hope no more,
2. So may we find un - fail - ing peace With love's unbounded store
3. We gath - er round the al - tar here, We oft have done be-fore,

We leave the out - er world for - lorn, And close the Chap-ter door.
And may our friend-ship here in-crease With - in the Chap-ter door.
And join our hands in un - ion dear With - in the Chap ter door.

Air—Coronation. Page 3.

1. Within our Chapter met again,
   With hearts and purpose strong,
We'll raise our notes of grateful praise,
   With union in our song.

2. Around our altar's sacred shrine,
   May love's pure incense rise,
Bearing upon its mystic flame
   Our music to the skies.

Air—Federal Street. Page 10.

1. Supreme Grand Patron! God of power,
Be with us in this happy hour:
Smile on our work, our plans approve,
Fill every heart with hope and love.

2. Let each discordant thought be gone,
And love unite our hearts in one;
May we in union strong combine,
In work and worship so divine.

Air—Hamburg. Page 10.

1. O come, loud anthems let us sing,
Loud anthems to our Almighty King;
For we our voices high should raise,
When our Salvation's Rock we praise,

2. O come, and bow before the Lord,
Ye who can best his praise record:
Come, and with holy hosts above,
Sing of the wonders of his love.

Air—Dennis. Page 8.

1. Lord in this evening hour
   We sisters here attend,
And bless thy love, and own thy pow'r,
   Our Father and our Friend.

2. Lord, may that holier day
   Dawn on thy servant's sight;
And purer worship may we pay
   In heaven's unclouded light.

BEETHOVEN. S. M.

Arr. from BEETHOVEN.

1. O Lord, thy per - fect word   Di - rects our steps a - right;
2. Ce - les - tial light it sheds,   To cheer this vale be - low;
3. True wis - dom it im - parts;   Commands our hope and fear;

Nor can all oth - er books af - ford Such pro - fit and de - light.
To dis - tant lands its glo - ry spreads, And streams of mer - cy flow.
O! may we hide it in our hearts, And feel its influ'nce there.

OLMUTZ. S. M.

Gregorian.

1. While my Re-deem-er's near, My Shep-herd and my Guide, I
2. To ev - er fra - grant meads, Where rich a - bun-dance grows, His
3. Dear Shepherd! if I stray, My wand'ring feet re - store; And

bid fare-well to ev - 'ry fear; My wants are all sup - plied.
gra cious hand in - dul-gent leads, And guards my sweet re - pose.
guard me with a watch - ful eye, And let me rove no more.

CARROLL. L. M.

Rob. Morris, LL. D.   J. R. Dunham.

1. In dew-y *Morn*, with day begun, The reddening east al-lures the sight ;
2. In gentle *Eve*, with parting day, The painted west rewards the gaze :
3. So Sisters of the Ris-ing Sun, May all your working hours be past

We see the mild, the Ris-ing Sun, And bless th'in-vig-or-at - ing light.
And when her last beams fade a-way We lin-ger o'er the gor-geous rays.
That when your tem-ple-toil is done Your brightest scenes may be your last.

MANOAH. C. M.

From G Rossini.

1. O God! we lift our hearts to thee, And grate-ful voic - es raise;
2. Here may our souls de-light to bless The God of truth and grace,
3. May each un - ho - ly pas-sion cease, Each e - vil tho't be crush'd,

We thank thee for this joy - ful day, Ac-cept our hum-ble praise.
Who crowns our la - bor with suc - cess, A mong the ris - ing race.
Each anx-ious care that mars our peace In Faith and Love be hushed.

DENNIS. S. M.

H. G. NAGELI.

1. Kind Fa-ther! hear our prayer, We bow be-fore thy throne;
2. With-in these walls may Peace And Har-mo-ny be found;

O may we find ac-cept-ance there, And peace be-fore un-known.
May Faith and Char-i-ty in-crease, And Hope and Love a-bound.

STATE STREET. S. M.

FAWCETT.

JONATHAN C. WOODMAN.

1. Blest be the tie that binds Our hearts in Chris-tian love;
2. Be-fore our Fath-er's throne We pour our fer-vent prayers;
3. A glorious hope re-vives Our cour-age by the way;

The fel-low-ship of kindred minds Is like to that a-bove.
Our fears, our hopes, our aims are one, Our comforts and our cares.
While each in ex-pec-ta-tion lives, And longs to see the day.

PRAISE. 6s & 4s, 8s & 6s.

Rob. Morris, LL.D.

Arr. by H. Tucker.

1. Be - gin the work of praise, The joys of song be - gin;
2. It tells of death-less Love, And Faith and Hope sub - lime;
3. Then let the song of praise Our eve - ning tasks be - gin;

And bid the mys - tic rays To en - ter in.......
It lifts the soul a - bove All things of time....
And bid the mys - tic rays To en - ter in.......

Chorus.

The gleam-ing light, The guid-ing light, The light that shines a - far:

It yields a radiance pure and bright, The beau-ti-ful, beau-ti-ful star.

HAMBURG. L. M.

BOWRING.

Arr. from Gregorian Chant.

1. On light-beams breaking from above, The'e - ter-nal course of mercy runs;
2. A - midst af-flic-tion's thick-est host, And sorrow's darkest, mightiest band,
3. O, be it ours to feel, to see, Thro' earth's perplexing scenes we roam

And by ten thou-sand cords of love Our heav'nly Fa - ther guides his sons.
The heav'nly cord is drawn the most, And most is felt the heav-'nly hand.
The cords that link us, God, to thee, And draw us to our fi - nal home.

FEDERAL STREET. L. M.

H. K. OLIVER.

1. Once more, O Lord, let grate-ful praise In songs of joy to thee as-cend;
2. Hear, then, our parting hymn of praise, And bind our hearts in love di-vine;

Thou art the Guardian of our days Our first and best and changeless Friend.
O may we walk in wis-dom's ways, And ev-er feel that we are thine.

ELEANORE. L. M. D.

WALTER H. JONES.

As from this place we go once more, Thy blessing, Father, we implore,

Still may we keep the heav'nly way, And strive to serve thee day by day.
D. S. Thy truth im-part, thy love dis-till, That we may know and do thy will.

And 'till a-gain we gather here, Help us to la-bor in thy fear;

Air—Retreat. Page 13.

1. Great God, as seasons disappear,
   And changes mark the rolling year,
   As time with rapid pinion flies,
   May every season make us wise.

2. Our harvest months have o'er us rolled,
   And filled our fields with waving gold,
   Our tables spread, our garners stored !
   Where are our hearts to praise the Lord ?

3. Prepare us, Lord, by grace divine,
   Like stars in heaven to rise and shine ;
   Then shall our happy souls above
   Reap the full harvest of thy love !

Air—Pleyel's Hymn. Page 29.

1. Called from labor to repose,
   Round our Star again we close,
   May its wondrous, radiant light
   Gleam through sorrow's darkest night.

2. One by one each link must fall,
   Death's stern mandate comes to all ;
   May our golden chain of Love
   Miss no links, when joined above.

4. Father! when Life's day shall close,
   Labyrinth passed, its cares and woes ;
   Bring us all with Thee to dwell,
   Where no more we bid—Farewell.

A. C. S. BARIO.

HAST THOU GLEANED WELL TO-DAY?

Dr. C. R. Blackall.   R. L.

1. The shad-ows are fall-ing, Swift clos-eth the day, I hear a voice call-ing, It
2. The day is de-part-ing, The dark-ness is here; Ah! why am I start-ling, While
3. The light is ap-pear-ing, The dark-ness is gone, For Je-sus is near-ing, And

seem-eth to say, Oh, soul! hast thou glean'd well to-day? In he world's har-vest
heart beats with fear, Soul! hast thou *not* glean'd well to-day? In the world's bus-y
ten-der His tone,— Oh, soul! in *my* might glean each day; When the har-vest is

field, With its full precious yield, Has it vain-ly appealed— Oh, soul! hast thou
throng, Hast thou failed to be strong, Weak-ly yield-ing to wrong, Oh, hast thou not
o'er, Shall be joy ev-er-more, If the sheaves at thy door Shall say, thou hast

Refrain,

gleaned well to - day? Hast thou gleaned............ Hast thou gleaned.......... Hast thou
gleaned well to - day?
filled well thy day?

Hast thou gleaned,   Hast thou gleaned,

gleaned,............ well to - day? Oh, soul! hast thou gleaned well to - day?

Hast thou gleaned, &c.

RETREAT. L. M.

T. HASTINGS.

1. Come, sis - ters, ere to-night we part, Join ev - 'ry voice and ev'ry heart;
2. Here, sis - ters, we may meet no more, But there is yet a hap-pier shore,
3. O! may his love, with sweet control, Bind ev - 'ry pas - sion of my soul;

One solemn hymn to God we'll raise, One closing song of grate-ful praise.
And there, released from toil and pain, Dear sisters, we shall meet a - gain.
Bid ev - 'ry vain de sire de-part, And dwell for-ev - er in my heart.

SICILIAN HYMN. 8s 7s & 4s.

MOZART.

1. Lord, dis - miss us with Thy bless-ing, Fill our hearts with joy and peace;
2. Thanks we give and ad - o - ra - tion, For the gos - pel's joy-ful sound;

Let us each, Thy love pos - sess-ing, Tri-umph in re - deem-ing grace;
Oh, re - fresh us, Oh, re - fresh us, Trav'ling thro' this wild - er - ness.
May the fruits of Thy sal - va - tion In our hearts and lives a - bound;
May thy pres-ence, May thy pres-ence With us ev - er - more be found.

GREENVILLE. 8s & 7s Double.

J. J. ROUSSEAU.

1. Heav'n-ly Fa-ther, grant thy bless-ing On the du-ties of the day, }
May thy love each soul pos-sess-ing, Shine up-on our on-ward way, }
2. May our hearts the les-sons pon-der, We have learned within this place, }
And our footsteps nev-er wan-der, Guid-ed by re-strain-ing grace. }

Guard our steps, and guide us ev-er, Make our way se-rene-ly bright;
Taught of Thee, oh, loving Fa-ther, We our tru-est wis-dom gain,

Friend must part from friend, but ne-ver May we lose thy heavenly light.
In the sun-shine of thy fa-vor, We, Thy child-ren, would re-main.

Parting.   *8s & 7s Double.*

1. We have met—and gladness round us
   Hath a band of beauty twined,
Love with genial smile hath bound us
   Heart to heart, and mind to mind.
Words of friendship have been spoken,
   Hands been clasped ne'er clasped before;
Be the friendship long unbroken,
   Tho' the hands be clasped no more !

2. We are parting—softly breathe it—
   Every low, sad farewell tone!
That each heart may catch and wreathe it
   With the gems it calls its own ;
True hands in each other pressing—
   Moistened eye and lingering heart—
Lips invoking God's rich blessing—
   Thus, O friends ! thus let us part.

HOME SWEET HOME. 11s.

Robt Morris.
Chorus or Duet.

Henry Tucker.

1. The Star we have followed now sinks in the west, But leaves in our
2. When called from earth's labor to lands far a - way, Where sor-row is

hearts all its mem - o - ries blest, As spring yields to sum-mer, yet
pleas-ure, and dark-ness is day, May all now de - part - ing in

fades not its bloom: So bear we these mem-o-ries joyful-ly home.
har-mo-ny come, And bloom in God's presence with angels at home.

Chorus.

Home, home, sweet, sweet home, We praise Thee, our Father, who giveth a home.

WHEN THE SCENE OF LIFE CHANGES.

JULIETTE T. BURTON.

Arr. by HENRY TUCKER.

1. When the scene of life changes from pleasure to gloom, And the soul sees its
2. This Eastern Star blends in its man-tle of light.   All the col-ors that

mid-night un-set by a ray, When the spirit droops low 'neath the weight of its
make up a pic-ture as bright   As char-i-ty, pa-tience, long-suff'ring and

doom, As the hopes that once lighted its halls die a-way, Then there shines thro' the
love, Can catch from the rap-ture of an-gels a-bove, As it shines thro' the

win-dows of heaven a-far, { Bright gleams that shed peace from a beautiful Star, }
                          { The "Star of the East," that most beautiful Star. }
win-dows of heaven a-far, { And we bless and adore thee, our beautiful Star, }
                          { Thou Star of the East, oh ! most beautiful Star. }

WEARY WANDERER.

Miss Fanny Crosby.   T. E. Perkins.

1. Wea-ry wan-d'rer o'er the main, Seek-ing for thy home a-gain,
2. Stranger, on a rock-y strand, Long-ing for thy fa-ther-land,
3. Lone-ly watcher, pale with grief, Thou shalt find a sweet re-lief,

Thro' the gath-'ring mists that rise, Vail-ing thy na-tal skies;
Thro' the gath-'ring clouds that rise, Vail-ing thy na-tal skies;
Tho' thy tears un-heed-ed fall, Heav-en will bless them all;

Look beyond, there's light for thee, Stream-ing o'er the tur-oid sea,
Look beyond, there's hope for thee, Dawn-ing o'er the tran-quil sea,
Look beyond, there's joy for thee, Break-ing o'er a troub-led sea,

Soft ly it smiles, tho' distant far, The beau-ti-ful East ern Star.

Doxology.

Praise God, from whom all blessings flow;
Praise him, all creatures here below;
Praise him above, ye heavenly throng;
Praise God, our Father, in our song.

MENDON.

1. Far from the world's cold strife and pride, Come join our peaceful, hap - py band;
2. Then may you in our la - bors join, And prove yourself a sis - ter true,

Come stranger, we your feet will guide, Where Truth and Love shall hold com-mand.
All sor-did, self - ish cares re - sign, And keep our sa-cred Truths in view.

JERUSALEM.

1. Spir - it of pow'r and might! be-hold Thy willing serv - ant here;
2. Tho' dark - some skies shall o'er her low'r, And dangers fill the way;

With Thy pro - tec - tion her in - fold, And free her heart from fear.
Sup - port her with Thy gracious pow'r, And be her con - stant stay.

MARY C. PRATT.

ZAIDA. 8s & 6s.

1. Our East-ern Star, whose quivering rays Re-flect-ed in the tear,
2. Our East-ern Star, that led the way, When patient, tremb-ling hands,
3. Our East-ern Star, whose rays of hope Give to the fair young queen,
4. Our East-ern Star, that ling-ered o'er A dear lov'd brother's Tomb,
5. Our East-ern Star, that still shines on, O'er sickness, pain and loss,

Of him whose vow made sac-ri-fice, Of that he held most dear,
Gathered the sheaves of bar-ley up, Left by a stern command!
Cour-age to plead a righteous cause Though dan-ger lay be-tween!
Where wait-ing hearts keep vig-ils lone In si-lence and in gloom!
That lights the way where burden-ed feet May rest be-neath the cross;

And lay be-neath the lift-ed veil Up-on the up-turned brow
That found within the heart a door Where Sym-pa-thy crept in,
That lift-ed up her heart to see, God in his might-y power,
Un-til in words of tend-er-ness The Master's voice was heard,
That draws up with its kindling rays In-to one band of love,

Of her whose brave clear voice re-plied, "Fath-er, ful-fill thy vow,"
For all who bend be-neath life's cares, In sor-row or in sin.
A pres-ent strength, a pres-ent help, In ev-'ry tri-al hour,
"Thy broth-er he shall live a-gain; Be-liev-est thou the word?"
And help us walk to-geth-er here To that dear home a-bove.

RATHBUN. 8s & 7s.

ROB. MORRIS, LL. D. J. CONKEY.

Ada. 1. Guide us up a-mong the mountains Where true Adah smiled at death;
Esther. 2. Land of Persia's queen im-mor-tal, Star of matchless wonder show;
Electa. 3. Where the rose of Shar-on bloom eth, By E-lec-ta's grave a-far,

Ruth. Lead us down be-side the foun tains, Sa-cred to Ruth's trust-ful faith
Martha. Thence with Mar-tha to the por-tal, Guiding our glad feet to go.
There in night-ly glo-ry com-eth, Gen-tly the bright EASTERN STAR!

DUKE STREET. L. M.

J. HATTON.

1. Far from the world's cold strife and pride, Come join our peaceful, happy band.
2. Then may you in our la-bors join, And prove yourself a sis-ter true;

Come, stranger, we your feet will guide, Where truth and love shall hold com mand.
All sor-did, sel fish cares resign, And keep our sa-cred Truths in view.

IDA. S. M.

Rob. Morris, LL D.   E. W. Dunbar.

Adah 1. Fair - est of Souls a - bove Are those who suf - fer'd here;
Ruth 2. A - mong the pearls of earth Most cher ished con - stan - cy,
Esther 3. Ten thousand anx - ious thoughts Do oft our pray'rs op-press;
Martha 4. And al - to - geth - er blest Are those who know the Lord:
Electa 5. Love - ly up on the shore Of Jordan's stream she stands,

They gave the sac - ri - fice of Love To prove their hearts sincere.
Maid of a high ce - les - tial birth, Child of e - ter - ni - ty!
But He who reign's in heav'nly courts Will sure-ly hear and bless.
The grave will kind-ly yield its guest To his re - sist - less word.
Who gave her life for Christ and bore His wit-ness in her hand.

Martha.   Air—Hurd.   Page 4.

1. Yea, I believe, although death's cloud
   Enwrap my soul in gloom;
   Thou art the Christ, the Son of God,
   The Savior that should come;—
   Yea, Lord, I *do* believe!

2. Yea, I believe; what though the grave
   Hath won my love from me;
   I felt that Thou hadst power to save,
   And still do trust in Thee;
   Yea, Lord, I *do* believe!

3. Yea, I believe; Lord, let this hour
   Some gracious token give!
   O, grant a sweet, reviving power,
   That others may believe;—
   Yea, Lord, I *do* believe!
                        Rob. Morris LL. D.

Electa.   Air—Woodland.   Page 25.

1. By her we learn the tenderest heart
   Is brav-st to endure;
   For at the Cross He'll not desert,
   Who all its sufferings bore.

2. Among ten thousand fairest she,
   When, bleeding, dying, high,
   Her risen Lord proclaimed her free,
   And hailed her to the sky.

3. Her fame, upon the wings of time,
   Through every land has swept;
   Electa's faith unmatched, sublime,
   Electa's name has kept.

4. Meek, radiant one! whose willing blood
   Her faith in Christ did seal,
   While hearts can throb, and tears be stirred,
   Thy history we will tell?
                        Rob Morris. LL. D.

CHANT NO. 1.

Reception.   Arr. by AGNES WILDT and KATIE SULLY, Rockford, Ill.   **Fine.**

Though I speak with the tongues of | men, and of | angels, | And have not charity, I am become as sounding | But the | brass and a | tinkling | cymbal.
D.C. And now abideth Faith | Hope, and | Charity; | | | greatest of | these is | Charity.

Esther.
And it was so, when the king saw Esther the Queen standing | in the | court, | That she obtained | favor — | in his | sight;
D.C. Then said the king unto her, What wilt | thou, Queen | Esther? | And what, what is thy request? it shall be even given thee to the | half — | of the | kingdom.

D. C.

Charity suffereth long, and is kind: charity | en - | vieth | not" | Rejoiceth not in iniquity. but re- | joic-eth | in the | truth.

And the king held out to Esther the golden scep- ter that was | in his | hand. | So Esther drew near, and touched the | t◡p — | of the | scepter.

CHANT NO. 2.

Adah.   Arr. by AGNES WILDT and KATIE SULLY, Rockford, Ill.

1. And Jephthah came to Mizpeh un- | to his | house, | And behold, his daughter came out to meet him, with tembrels and with | dances,
2. "And it came to pass, when he saw her that he rent his clothes and said, | Alas, my | daughter: | Thou hast brought me very low. and thou art one of them that | trouble me;

Electa.
Grace be with you, mercy, and peace, from | God the | Father, | And now I beseech thee, lady, not as tho' I wrote a new commandment unto | thee,

And she was his For I have opened my mouth un- | on - ly to the | child; Lord, | Beside her he had neither And I | son nor cannot go | daughter. back.

But that which we had from the begin- ning, that we | love one an- | other; | And this is love, that we walk after | his com- | mandments

CHANT NO. 3.

After O.   WALTER H. JONES.

1. Happy is the man that	findeth	wisdom,	And the man that	get - teth	un - der-	standing.
2. She is more precious	than	rubies,	And all the things thou canst desire are not to be com-	par - ed	un - to	her.
3. Her ways are	ways of	pleasantness,	And	all her	paths are	peace.

CHANT NO. 4.

Ruth.   WALTER H. JONES,

And behold Boaz came from Beth-lehem : and said unto the reap-ers, the	Lord be	with you.	And they answered him,	The	Lord —	bless thee.
Then said Boaz unto his servants that was set	over the	reapers,	Whose	dam-	sel is	this ?
And the servant that was set over the reapers	answered and	said,	It is the Moabitish dam-sel that came back with Naomi out of the	coun-try	of —	Moab.

CHANT NO. 5.

Martha   WALTER H. JONES.

1. Then said Martha	un - to	Jesus,	Lord, if thou had'st been here my	brother	had not	died.
2. But I know that	e - ven	now	Whatsoever thou will ask of God,	God will	give it	thee.
3. Jesus saith	un - to	her,	Thy brother	shall	rise a-	gain.
4. Martha saith	un - to	him,	I know that he shall rise again in the resurrection	at the	last	day.
5. Jesus saith unto her, I am the resurrection,	and the	life	He that believeth in me, though he were	dead, yet	shall he	live.
6. And whosoever	liv-	eth	And believeth in	me shall	never	die.

THE LORD'S PRAYER.

Ritual, page 58.   Gregorian Chant.

1. { Our Father, who art in heaven,	hallowed be thy name;	{ Thy Kingdom come, Thy will be done, on }	earth, as it is in heav'n;

2. Give us this | day, our | daily | bread ;
And forgive us our trespasses, as we forgive | them that | tres-pass a- | gainst us.
3. And lead us not into temptation, but de- | liv - er | us from | evil ;
For thine is the Kingdom, and the power, and the | glory, for- | ever. A- | men;

WELCOME.

Ritual, pages 38 and 65.

WM. B. BRADBURY.

1. Wel-come, Sis-ter, to our Or - der, By the al - tar now bow down,
2. Wel-come, Sis-ter, to our Chap - ter, We shall need your help and care

There re - ceive the Ob - li - ga - tion, Will - ing heart and pur - pose strong,
In the har-vest field of la - bor You shall have a right-ful share,

Join a band of faith-ful sis - ters Bound by love and char - i - ty,
Wel-come, wel-come, hea-ven bless you, Wel-come, wel-come is our prayer,

Here we'll greet you as a sis - ter Glad - ly free -ly meet you here.
Wel-come wel-come gen-tle sis - ter Wel - come, wel - come to you here.

Air—Frederick. Page 26.

1. Approach not the altar with gloom in thy soul,
Nor let thy feet falter, from terrors control!
God loves not the sadness of fear and mistrust:
O serve him with gladness, the Gracious and Just.

2. Nor come to the altar with pride in thy mien;
But lowly and simple, in courage serene:
Bring meekly, before him, the faith of a child;
Bow down and adore him, with heart undefiled.

HEBER. C. M.

GEORGE KINGSLEY.

1. By cool Si-lo-am's shad-y rill, How fair the li-ly grows!
2. By cool Si-lo-am's shad-y rill The li-ly must de-cay;
3. O Thou, who giv-est life and breath, We seek thy grace a-lone,

How sweet the breath beneath the hill, Of Shar-on's dew-y rose!
The rose that blooms be-neath the rill Must short ly fade a-way.
In childhood, manhood, age and death, To keep us still thine own.

WOODLAND. C. M.

W. B. TAPPAN,

N. D. GOULD

1. There is an hour of peaceful rest, To mourning wand'rers given; There is a joy for
2. There is a home for weary souls, By sin and sorrow driven—When toss'd on life's tem-
3. There fra-grant flow'rs immortal bloom, And joys supreme are giv'n; There rays divine dis-

souls distressed, A balm for ev-ery wounded breast: 'Tis found a-bove—in heaven.
pestuous shoals, Where storms arise, and o-cean rolls, And all is drear—but heaven.
perse the gloom; Be-yond the con-fines of the tomb Ap-pears the dawn of heaven

FREDERICK. 11s.

GEO. KINGSLEY.

1. I would not live al-way; I ask not to stay, Where storm af-ter storm ris es dark o'er the way; I would not live al - way; no, wel-come the tomb; Since Je-sus hath lain there, I dread not its gloom.

2. Who, who would live alway, a - way from his God, A - way from yon heav-en, that bliss - ful a - bode, Where the riv - ers of pleas - ure flow o'er the bright plains, And the noon-tide of glo - ry e - ter-nal - ly reigns.

3. Where the saints of all a - ges in harmony meet, Their Sav - ior and brethren trans-port-ed to greet, While the an - thems of rap - ture un- ceas-ing - ly roll, And the smile of the Lord is the life of the soul!

Air—Heber. Page 25.

1. Calm on the bosom of thy God,
   Young spirit rest thee now,
E'en while with us our footsteps trod,
   His seal was on thy brow.

2. Lone are the paths, and sad the bowers,
   Whence thy meek smile is gone;
But oh! a brighter home than ours,
   heaven is now thine own.

Air—Naomi. Page 31.

1. Here death his sacred seal hath set
   On bright and by-gone hours;
The dead we mourn are with us yet,
   And more than ever—ours!

2. By them, though holy hope and love,
   We feel, in hours serene,
Connected with that home above,
   Immortal and unseen

HOLLEY. 7s.

Geo. Hews.

1. Wreathe the mourning badge a-round, Sis-ters, pause! a funeral sound!
2. How her life-path has been trod, Sis-ters, leave we un-to God!
3. Here a-midst the things that sleep, Let her rest—her grave is deep;
4. Dust to dust, the dark de cree—Soul to God, the soul is free!

Where the part-ed had a home, Meet and bear her to the tomb.
Friend ship's man-tle, love and faith, Lend sweet fragrance e'en to death.
D·ath has triumph'd, lov-ing hands Can not raise her from her bands.
Leave her with the lone-ly lain—Sis-ters, we shall meet a-gain!

ROCK OF AGES. 7s.

Toplady.

Dr. Thomas Hastings.

Fine.

1. Rock of A-ges, cleft for me, Let me hide my-self in thee,
D. C. Be of sin the dou-ble cure; Cleanse me from its guilt and pow'r.

D.C.

Let the wa-ter and the blood, From thy riv-en side which flowed

2. While I draw this fleeting breath,
   When mine eyelids close in death,
   When I soar to worlds unknown,

See thee on thy judgment throne,
Rock of Ages, cleft for me,
Let me hide myself in thee.

REST. L. M.

Wm, Bradbury.

1. Asleep in Je - sus! blessed sleep! From which none ever wake to weep;
2. Asleep in Je - sus! peaceful rest ! Whose waking is su-preme-ly blest,
3. Asleep in Je - sus! far from thee Thy kindred and their graves may be:

A calm and un-dis-turbed re-pose, Un-brok-en by the last of foes.
No fear, no woe, shall dim the hour That man-i-fests the Sav-ior's power.
But thine is still a   blessed sleep From which none ever wake to weep.

ZEPHYR. L. M.

William B. Bradbury.

1. Why should we weep and mourn for her Whose place will know her here no more?
2. How man - y wear-y days on earth, How many griefs, they numbered o'er,
3. Dear is the spot where Christians sleep, And sweet the strain which angels pour,

Released from all life's hurt-ful foes, She is not lost, but gone be - fore.
She now en joys a heaven-ly birth ; She is not lost, but gone be - fore.
O why should we in an-guish weep? She is not lost, but gone be - fore.

PLEYEL'S HYMN. 7s.

J. PLEYEL.

1. Soft-ly, sad - ly, bear her forth   To her dark and sil - ent bed;
2. This our sis - ter gone be-fore,   May we in   remembrance keep;
3. One last look— one parting sigh,   Ah, too sad   for words to   tell;

Weep not that she's lost to earth,   Weep not that her spir-it's fled.
Hop-ing, as time pass - es o'er,   We shall meet where none e'er weep.
Yet, though tears may dim each eye,   Hope we still, and sigh fare - well.

WINDHAM. L. M.

WATTS.

DANIEL READ

1. Un - vail thy bos-om, faithful tomb! Take this new treasure to thy trust;
2. Nor pain, nor grief, nor an-xious fear, Invade thy bounds; no mor-tal woes
3. Break from his throne, illustrious morn! Attend, O earth, his sovereign word!

And give these sa-cred rel-ics room To slum-ber in the   si-lent dust.
Can reach the si-lent sleepers here, While angels watch the   soft re-pose.
Re-store thy trust; a glorious form Shall then as-cend to meet the Lord.

REQUIEM. S. H. M.

T. HASTINGS.

1. Friend af - ter friend de - parts, Who has not lost a friend?
2. There is a world a - bove, Where part - ing is un - known;

There is no u - nion here of hearts That finds not here an end;
A whole e - ter - ni - ty of love Formed for the good a - lone;

Were this frail world our on - ly rest, Liv-ing or dying, none were blest.
And faith beholds the dy - ing here Trans-lat-ed to that hap pier sphere.

MOUNT VERNON. 8s. & 7s.

Slow and soft.

MASON.

1. *Sister*, thou wast mild and lovely,
Gentle as the summer breeze,
Pleasant as the air of evening
When it floats along the trees.

2. Peaceful be thy silent slumber,
Peaceful, in the grave so low;
Thou no more wilt join our number,
Thou no more our songs shalt know.

3. Dearest *sister*, thou hast left us,
Here thy loss we deeply feel;
But 'tis God that hath bereft us,
He can all our sorrows heal.

4. Yet again we hope to meet thee,
When the day of life is fled,
Then, in heaven, we hope to greet thee,
Where no farewell tear is shed.

NAOMI. C. M.

Dr. L. Mason.

1. Think gen-tly of the erring one! O do not thou for - get,
2. Speak gen-tly to the erring one! Thou yet may'st win her back,
3. For - get not thou hast often sinn'd, And sin - ful yet may be;

How - ev - er dark-ly stain'd by sin, She is thy sis - ter yet.
With ho - ly words and tones of love, To vir - tues pleasant track?
Deal gen-tly with the err-ing heart, As God has dealt with thee!

PETERBORO'. C. M.

R. Harrison.

1. Ac cept the trust we of - fer thee, Our { Ma - tron / Pa - tron } and our guide;
2. Oh! lead us by the light of truth, To walk in wis dom's way,

May jus-tice, truth, and pur pose high, In all thy pow'rs a - bide.
Thro' all the try - ing paths of life, To realms of end - less day.

ADAIR. 6s. & 4s.

Rob. Morris, LL. D.

1. Gone to the shad ow-land, Ne'er to re - turn; Blent with the spir-it-band;
2. Sweet are the tho'ts of her, Tho' she is gone; Rays from the sep-ul-cher;
3. See from yon world afar, Where she hath gone, Bright beams the Eastern Star;

Why should we mourn? Scaped from the toil and pain, Cleans'd from the
Why should we mourn? Gen - tle the words she said, Bright'ning the
Why should we mourn? Star in whose ho - ly ray, Love, truth and

earth - ly stain, Why yield to sor-row's stain? Why should we mourn?
path we tread, Blest is the hal-lowed dead; Why should we mourn?
hope dis-play, Point the ce - les - tial day; Why should we mourn?

Air—Bethany. 6s & 4s.

1. Nearer, my God, to thee,
Nearer to thee!
E'en though it be a cross
That raiseth me!
Still all my song shall be,
Nearer, my God, to thee
Nearer, my God, to thee
Nearer to thee.

2. Or, if on joyful wing,
Cleaving the sky,
Sun, moon, and stars forgot,
Upward I fly,
Still all my song shall be,
Nearer, my God, to thee,
Nearer, my God, to thee,
Nearer to thee.

Sarah F. Adams.

BOYLSTON. S. M.

WATTS. Dr. LOWELL MASON.

1. The pit-y of the Lord, To those that fear His name, Is
2. Our days are as the grass, Or like the morn-ing flow'r; If
3. But Thy com-pas-sions, Lord, To end-less years en-dure; And

such as ten-der par-ents feel: He knows our fee-ble frame.
one sharp blast sweep o'er the field, It with-ers in an hour.
children's chil-dren ev-er find Thy words of prom-ise sure.

WARD. L. M.

MONTGOM'RY. Dr. L. MASON.

1. Faith, hope, and char-i-ty, these three, Yet is the great-est char-i-ty;
2. Faith, that in pray-er can never fail, Hope, that o'er doubting must pre-vail,
3. The morning-Star is lost in light, Faith van-ish-es at per-fect sight,
4. But char-i-ty, se-rene, sub-lime. Be-yond the reach of death and time,

Fathers of Lights, these gifts im-part To mine and ev-ery hu-man heart.
And char-i-ty, whose name a-bove Is God's own name, for God is Love.
The rainbow pass-es with the storm, And hope with sorrow's fad-ing form.
Like the blue sky's all bound-ing space, Holds heav'n and earth in its em-brace.

ST. THOMAS. S. M.

WATTS.   A. WILLIAMS.

1. The Lord my shep-herd is; I shall be well sup-plied;
2. He leads me to the place Where heav'n-ly pas-ture grows,
3. The boun-ties of thy love Shall crown my fu-ture days;

Since he is mine, and I am His, What can I want be-side?
Where liv-ing wa-ters gent-ly pass, And full sal-va-tion flows.
Nor from Thy house will I re-move, Nor cease to speak Thy praise.

ARLINGTON. C. M.

DR. ARNE.

1. There is a star, a love-ly star, That lights the dark-est gloom;
2. There is a voice, a cheering voice, That lifts the soul a-bove;
3. That voice is heard from Zi-on's height And speaks the soul for-given.

And sheds a peace-ful ra-di'nce o'er The pros-pects of the tomb.
Dis-pels dis-trust-ful, anxi-ous doubts, And whispers God is love.
That star is rev-el-a-tions light That hope the hope of heav'n.

Reception. Air.—Arlington. Page 34.

1. Of thee, Supreme Grand Power above'
   We ask that Wisdom sure
   Which will direct our work of Love
   And make its teachings pure,

2. Which will the way illume with light'
   And help each weary heart,
   The lessons true to read aright,
   Which our star's rays impart.

After Adah.

3. May we, like Adah, ever prize
   A stainless record white,
   We, then, unveiled, can lift our eyes,
   Though facing Heaven's own light.

After Ruth.

4. The Master calleth some to reap,
   Some humbly glean the grain ;
   The faithful, working, tho' they weep,
   Ne'er find their labor vain.

After Esther.

5. With Persia's noble Queen we stand
   In truth's victorious might,
   And fearlessly, with heart and hand,
   Defend the cause of Right !

After Martha.

6. Our Hope in God, our trustful Faith
   In Immortality
   Shall brighten Life, shall conquer Death
   And face Eternity !

After Electa.

7. While Higher Power shall now impart
   New Lights on precepts true,
   May symbol sweet, instruct each heart,
   Till we this lesson view.

8. That when life's teachings here we leave,
   Though harsh they seem to prove,
   We'll from the Source of Light receive
   Their meanings, fraught with Love.
   A. C. S. BARIO.

Air—Stephens. Page 5.

1. Spirit of power and might ! behold
   Thy willing servant here ;
   With thy protection her infold,
   And free her heart from fear.

2. Though darksome skies shall o'er her
   And danger filled the way ; [lower,
   Support her with thy gracious power,
   And be her constant stay.

Air—Peterboro'. Page 31.

1. There is a Star of beaming light,
   A gem divinely dear, [night,
   Oh! bring new rays, dear Friends, to
   These yearning hearts to cheer.

2. Oh! name once more the fond, the true,
   The heroines of the star !
   Their deeds enkindle us anew,
   And bear our souls afar.

3. And light the gloomy path below,
   Sweet words of comfort bring ;
   Dear Friends, we greet you warmly now,
   And "Welcome ! welcome !" sing.
   ROB. MORRIS, LL. D.

Opening. Air—Manoah. Page 7.

1. With earnest hearts and willing hands,
   Within our Chapter room,
   We meet a warm fraternal band,
   Our labors to resume.

2. To aid each other on the way,
   Through mazes dark and drear ;
   While o'er us all, the golden ray
   Of Bethlehem's Star, shines clear.

3. That Star which shall the faithful guide
   Though long and drear the road,
   To gild, at life's fair eventide
   The city of our God ! A C. S. BARIO.

Adah. Air.— The Prairie Flower.

1. O ! the grand deliverance of the moun-
      tain maid ! [said ;
   "Keep the vow, my father"—thus she
   "Shall the Mason's daughter fear for
      truth to die ?
   There's a home beyond the sky.
   CHO.—Gone from the mountain—lost to
      her home.—
      Called in life's beauty to the tomb ;
      Wake the wild lamenting in the lone-
      She would never come again. [ly glen

Electa. Air.—No One to Love.

1. Land far away, home of the blest.
   Mansion Celestial, O give her sweet rest!
   With her Beloved, crowned with His crown
   Bathed in His glory, whose cross she has
      borne ;
   No failing tongue, no fading eye,
   No worldly scorn, or heart-rending sigh.
   Land far away.—etc.

MISSIONARY HYMN. 7s & 6s.

Arr. by JENNIE E. MATHEWS.
From Level and Square by ROB. MORRIS, LL. D.

DR. LOWELL MASON.

1. We meet up-on the lev-el, We part up-on the square; What words of precious
2. We meet up-on the lev-el, Tho' from ma-ny stations come; We hail these yearly
3. We part when the chapter clos-es, For the world must have its due; We min-gle with the

mean-ing, These words, Ma-son-ic, are, Come, let us con-tem-plate them; They're
gath'-rings And glad-ly leave our home, We all should leave our worldly cares Out-
multi-tude A cold un-friend-ly crew. But the in-fluence of these gath'-rings In our

wor-thy of a thought; With the purest, and the tru-est, And the rar-est they are fraught.
side our Chapter door, With joy to meet each sis-ter, Up-on the check-ered floor.
mem-'ry is green, And we hail the joy-ous spring-time To re-new the hap-py scene.

4. There's a world where all are equal;
   (We're hurrying toward it fast)
   Where we shall meet all loved ones
   When the gates of death are past.
   We shall meet our heavenly Patron,
   And it bids us all prepare
   To bear with us some offering
   Glean'd from the Eastern Star.

5. We shall meet in happy homes
   And ne'er again shall part;
   There's a mansion surely ready
   For each trusting faithful heart.
   There's a mansion and a welcome
   And a multitude is there,
   Who have met upon the earth below
   As they'll meet again up there.

6. Let us meet in love and friendship,
   While laboring patient here;
   Let us meet and let us labor
   Though the labor seem severe.
   Already in the Western sky
   A sign bids us prepare
   To meet once more those loved ones
   And ne'er again know care.

7. Hands 'round then, faithful sisters,
   Form the bright, fraternal chain;
   Although broken here below,
   Shall be joined in heaven again.
   Oh, what words of precious meaning
   And what comfort, too, they bear;
   We part upon the earth below
   To meet again up there.

BERA. L. M.

J. E. GOULD.

1. Now we are met from distant parts, Be joined in one our gladdened hearts;
2. May this a type and em - blem be Of that great meet-ing all shall see,
3. O Thou who touched with living fire The prophet's lips, our tho'ts in-spire;

May all we do be done in love, Like those who meet to praise above.
Where truth di vine tunes ev-'ry chord In har-mo-ny with Christ the Lord.
And grant the grace which still controls The aims and words of lov - ing souls.

STOCKWELL.

CLOSING.

1. Part in peace! with deep thanksgiving, Off'ring as we homeward tread,
2. Part in peace! such are the praises, God, our Mak-er, lov-eth best;

Gracious service to the liv-ing, Tranquil mem'ry to the dead.
Such the worship that up - rais-es Human hearts to heav'n ly rest.

OPENING AND CLOSING ODES.

(Inscribed to Burns Chapter, Ore.)

NELLIE R. GRACE.   AMERICA.   HENRY CAREY.

Opening.
1. Star of the East! arise! Guide where our duty lies, Bright Star above! Oh, may our
2. In shadow of thy wing, An-gel of peace we sing, Thy song of love. Oft - en and
Closing.
1. Gently in gold en West, Sinketh our Star to rest A-dieu! a - dieu! Now with our

meeting be Type of sweet harmony, Sis - ters and brothers, we Shall reign in love.
oft, a-gain, Sing we thy glad refrain, "Peace on earth, good will to man!" Thy song of love.
labors done. Turn we toward setting sun, As links drop one by one, A - dieu! a - dieu!

GREETING.—ANOTHER LINK.

Air:—"RED, WHITE AND BLUE."

A welcome, a welcome we're giving—
We, brothers and sisters are—
To you, who with us, are receiving
The guidance of Bethlehem's Star.
The Lion, the Lamb, and the Lily,
The Sun and the Bible, too,

Are symbols of virtuous living
In rays of our red, white and blue.

In th' rays of the red, white and blue;
In th' rays of the golden and green:
Oh, these are our colors and symbols—
The beauties of Masonry's queen.

WELCOME.

ARR. NELLIE GRACE.   *(Inscribed to Electa Chapter, Girard, Ks.)*   FROM VON WEBER.

1st voice.—Star of our Or-der, Bright, mystic Star, Glad-ly we hail thee, Shining a - far.
1st voice.—A - dah, E-lec - ta, Mar-tha and Ruth, Es-ther, the queenly, Lecture with Truth

2d v.—Soon as thou shinest Out on the air, Borne by the light breeze, Floateth our pray'r—
2d v.—Rest from your labors, Daughters of toil, Night closes o'er us Rest we a-while.

Both—Floateth, floateth our pray'r—
Both— Rest we, rest we a - while.

Both { "Welcome our Sister! welcome her here, Watch o'er her kindly Points of our Star;
Light thou her pathway, Bright Eastern Star! Light thou her journey, Bright Eastern } Star!"
Both { "Welcome! oh, welcome! ye Sister friend! This is thy greeting, Signaled a-far;
Mystic rites of Star to ye extended!" Star of our Order, Bright Eastern } Star!

CLOSING.

MISSIONARY CHANT.

1. As from this place we go once more, Thy blessing, Father, we im-plore;
2. And till a-gain we gather here, Help us to la-bor in Thy fear;

Still may we keep the heav'nly way, And strive to serve Thee day by day.
Thy Truth impart, Thy Love dis-till, That we may know and do Thy will.

MALVERN. L. M.

Dr. L. Mason.

1. Fa-ther! a-dored in worlds a bove, Thy glorious name be hallowed still;
2. Lord! make our daily wants thy care; For-give the sins that we for-sake;
3. E-vils be-set us ev-'ry hour; Thy kind pro-tec-tion we im-plore:

Thy kingdom come with pow'r and love, And earth, like heav'n, o-bey thy will.
And as we in thy kindness share, Let fel-low-men of ours par-take.
Thine is the kingdom, thine the pow'r, Be thine the glo-ry ev-er-more!

LORRAINE.

ROB. MORRIS, LL. D.   J. R. DUNHAM.

1. Soft comes the morn-ing,   balm-y dews af-fuse the   rose;
2. When from the gloam-ing,   wea-ry hearts are bid   to   rise,

Hushed is the night bird in a soft re-pose; Soft comes the morning,
And light ce-les-tial cheers the dying eyes, When from the gloaming,

balmy dews af-fuse the rose;Hushed is the night bird in a soft re-pose;
weary hearts are bid to rise, And light ce-les-tial cheers the dy ing eyes

Far   be-yond the moun-tains, o'er the   murk-y fleece a-far,
Then   be-yond the moun-tains, o'er the   murk-y fleece a-far,

LORRAINE---Concluded.

Chorus.

Lo, in wondrous glory, lifts the Eastern Star. Star of the Sav-ior,
Lift in life e-ter-nal, lift the Eastern Star. Star, etc.

Repeat pp

guide the soul from sin a-far, Star of good o-men, 'tis the Eastern Star.

MATHEWS. L. M.

C. E. LESLIE.

1. Bright Star of Hope, we fol-low thee ; Herald divine we catch thy voice;
2. Hail, Star of Hope! our hearts adore Thy light, which shines on life's darkwave
3. Hail, Star of Hope! man's cer-tain Guide To truth and life by mer-cy given;

Thy notes pro-claim God's ju-bi-lee, And bid a ransomed world re-joice.
Like the bright guide on o-cean shore, The storm spent mar-i-ner to save.
Spread wide thy rays, till all man-kind Receive this richest boon of Heaven.

ITALIAN HYMN. 6s & 4s

Rob. Morris, LL. D.   F. Giardini.

1. God bless our glo - rious Star; Long may it   beam   a - far!
2. Re - ful - gent light di - vine,   O nev - er cease   to   shine
3. Let all who love its light, In joy - ous strains u - nite,

God bless our   Star. Give us this   brill - iant light, To guide by
Up - on this land! Wis dom in   thee we find, Beau - ty and
To praise our   Star. Long may it bright - ly gleam, Queen of the

day or night, Like Is - rael's Pil - lars bright, God bless our Star.
strength combin'd, With friends to - geth - er join'd, In heart and hand.
az - ure stream, Ech - o the oliss - ful theme, God bless our Star.

Initiation. Sweet Hour of Prayer. Rit. p. 58.

Sweet hour of prayer, sweet hour of
      prayer,
That calls me from a world of care,
And bids me, at my Father's throne,
Make all my wants and wishes known!
In seasons of distress and grief,
My soul has often found relief,
And oft escaped the tempter's snare,
By thy return sweet hour of prayer.

Dedication. Air—Duke Street. Page 20.

1. Thou hast thy temple, Lord of all,
      Where'er thy light and glory shine;
   While suns and stars before thee fall,
      And own thy majesty divine.

2. Lord! in thy sight completed stands
      This temple to thy truth and grace,
   And now we lift our hearts and hands
      To thee, to consecrate the place

WEBB. 7s. & 6s.

(Garfield's Favorite Hymn.)   Webb.

1. Ho, reap - ers of life's har - vest! Why stand with rust - ed blade
2. Thrust in your sharpened sick - le, And gath - er in the grain;
3. Mount up the heights of wis - dom, And crush each er - ror low;

Un - til the night draws round thee And day be - gins to fade?
The night is fast ap-proach - ing, And soon will come a - gain.
Keep back no words of knowl-edge That human hearts should know.

Why stand ye i - dle, wait - ing For reap - ers more to come?
The Mas - ter calls for reap - ers, And shall He call in vain?
Be faith - ful to thy mis - sion In ser - vice of thy Lord,

The gold - en morn is pass - ing Why sit ye i - dle, dumb!
Shall sheaves lie there, un - gath - ered, And waste up - on the plain?
And then a gold - en chap - let Shall be thy just re - ward.

HAPPY GREETING TO ALL.

Allegretto.

Arr. by H, WATERS.

1. Come, sis - ters, and join in our fes - ti - val song, And hail the sweet
2. Our Fa - ther in heav - en, we lift up to thee, Our voice of thanks-
3. And if, ere this glad year has drawn to a close, Some loved one a-
4. And now, as we part, let us bid all good cheer, We pray for a

joys which this day brings a - long, We'll join our glad voic - es in
giv - ing, our glad ju - bi - lee; Oh, bless us, and guide us, dear
mong us in death shall re - pose, Grant, Lord, that the spir - it in
bless - ing on our la-bors here; May man - y "bright jew - els" be

one hymn of praise, To God who has kept us, and lengthened our days.
Sav - ior, we pray, That from thy blest precepts we nev - er may stray.
heav - en may dwell, In the bos - om of Je - sus, where all shall be well.
add - ed in love, And "crowns of re - joic-ing, in man-sions a - bove.

Chorus

Hap - py greet-ing to all! Hap - py greet-ing to all!

Hap - py greet-ing.....................to all!

Hap - py greet-ing, hap - py greet - ing. hap - py greet-ing to all!

WELCOME GREETING.

Selected by ANNA E. GRAUL.

1 Wel-come, wel-come, wel-come is this meet-ing, Which with joy has filled each breast;
2. Cheer-ful, cheer-ful, cheer-ful be each per-son, Met a pleas-ant hour to spend;

Friends, ac-cept our hon - est greet-ing, Wel-come here to ev-'ry guest;
Let the song be sweet and mel-low, Here in har - mo-ny we blend;

Life has not a great-er treas-ure Than the friends whose love we gain;
Life is ev - er worth en-joy-ing, With a friend whose heart is true;

Fine

Ab-sence pains, but sweet-er is the pleas - ure, When at last we meet a - gain,
Care be-gone, no more, no more an-noy - ing, Friend-ship, here we treas-ure you.
D. s. May we ev - er thus u - nite to-geth - er, And on - ly but to meet a - gain.

D, S,

Wel-come, wel-come, now we all re - joice, With cheer - ful heart and voice.
Wel-come, wel-come, now we all re - joice, With cheer - ful heart and voice.

INSTALLATION ODE.

Rob. Morris. (*Composed expressly for this work.*)   English.

1. Hail to the East so light, Ay, hail to the chief e-lect! In ac-
2. Hail to the West so fair, Ay, hail to the Ma-tron's aid! In her
3. Hail to the South so true, Our Star in the gold-en day, And a
4. Hail to the Mys-tic Band, The pride of the East-ern Star! In the

claim to the ma-tron bright, With the badge of her rank be-deck'd
heart there is no de-spair, And she will not be dis-mayed,
loud ac-claim to you, For your charge you will not be-tray!
might of the Lord we stand, And we lift our pray-ers a-far,

A-round her we hast-en, In friend-ship sin-cere Each sis-ter and
For lo, on the Al-tar, The Book meets her eye, She nev-er will
The chain that you strengthen, From East un-to West, Oh may it still
That He will ce-ment us, In peace to com-bine, Each gift he hath

ma-son, In bonds so strong and dear. Then hail to the East so light. Ay,
fal-ter, With hope and truth so nigh. Then hail to the West so fair, Ay,
lengthen, Till all the earth is blest! Then hail to the South so true, Our
lent us, To use as if di-vine. Then hail to the Mys-tic Band, The

hail to the chief e-lect! An ac-claim to the Ma-tron bright, With the badge of her rank be-
hail to the Matron's aid! In her heart there is no de-spair, And she will not be dis-
Star in the gold-en day, And a loud acclaim to you For your charge you will not be-
pride of the Eastern Star, In the might of the Lord we stand, And we lift our pray-ers a-

INSTALLATION ODE---Concluded.

deck'd All hail, All hail, Sis - ters, Broth-ers, all hail, all hail.
may'd, All hail, All hail, Sis - ters, Broth-ers, all hail, all hail.
tray, All hail, All hail, Sis - ters, Broth-ers, all hail, all hail.
far! All hail, All hail, Sis - ters, Broth-ers, all hail, all hail.

AMERICA. 6s. & 4s.

S F. SMITH.   HENRY CAREY.

1. My coun - try! 'tis of thee, Sweet land of lib - er - ty,
2. My na - tive coun - try! thee, Land of the no - ble free,
3. Let mu - sic swell the breeze, And ring from all the trees
4. Our Fa - ther's God! to thee,—Au - thor of lib - er - ty!

Of thee I sing: Land where my fa - thers died, Land of the
Thy name I love; I love thy rocks and rills, Thy woods and
Sweet freedom's songs; Let mor - tal tongues a-wake, Let all that
To thee we sing; Long may our land be bright, With freedom's

Pil-grims' pride, From ev - 'ry moun - tain side Let free - dom ring!
tem - pled hills; My heart with rap - ture thrills, Like that a - bove.
breathe partake; Let rocks their si - lence break, The sound pro - long.
ho - ly light—Pro - tect us by thy might, Great God, our King.

INDEX.

TUNES.

FIRST LINES.

www.ingramcontent.com/pod-product-compliance
Lightning Source LLC
Chambersburg PA
CBHW060523280326
41933CB00014B/3082